Hebrews

'Insightful, pastoral, warm and encouraging. Charles has a gift for mining the gold and making it glitter.'
Martin Salter, Associate Pastor, Grace Community Church, Bedford

'These daily devotional readings will help Christians to understand and enjoy the book of Hebrews, and to rejoice afresh in the Lord Jesus Christ and all that he has done for them. Charles Price unpacks the Old Testament typology of the letter with brevity and clarity, and shows how the truths it teaches strengthen our faith and apply to our daily lives. Anyone who uses this guide will be blessed and motivated to press on in the Christian life with eyes firmly fixed on the eternal glory to come.'
John Stevens, National Director, Fellowship of Independent Evangelical Churches

30-DAY DEVOTIONAL

Hebrews

Charles Price
with Elizabeth McQuoid

FOOD
FOR THE
JOURNEY

INTER-VARSITY PRESS
36 Causton Street, London SW1P 4ST, England
Email: ivp@ivpbooks.com
Website: www.ivpbooks.com

First published 2017

British Library Cataloguing-in-Publication Data
A catalogue record for this book is available from the British Library.

ISBN: 978–1–78359–611–9
eBook ISBN: 978–1–78359–612–6

Typeset in Great Britain by CRB Associates, Potterhanworth, Lincolnshire
Printed in Great Britain by Ashford Colour Press Ltd, Gosport, Hampshire

Inter-Varsity Press publishes Christian books that are true to the Bible and that communicate the gospel, develop discipleship and strengthen the church for its mission in the world.

IVP originated within the Inter-Varsity Fellowship, now the Universities and Colleges Christian Fellowship, a student movement connecting Christian Unions in universities and colleges throughout Great Britain, and a member movement of the International Fellowship of Evangelical Students. Website: www.uccf.org.uk. That historic association is maintained, and all senior IVP staff and committee members subscribe to the UCCF Basis of Faith.

Preface

Can you guess how many sermons have been preached from the Keswick platform? Almost 6,500!

For over 140 years the Keswick Convention in the English Lake District has welcomed gifted expositors from all over the world. The convention's archive is a treasure trove of sermons preached on every book of the Bible.

This series is an invitation to mine that treasure. It takes the Bible Reading series given by well-loved Keswick speakers, past and present, and reformats them into daily devotionals. Where necessary, the language has been updated but, on the whole, it is the message you would have heard had you been listening in the tent on Skiddaw Street. Each day of the devotional ends with a newly written section designed to help you apply God's Word to your own life and situation.

Whether you are a convention regular or have never been to Keswick, this Food for the Journey series is a unique opportunity to study the Scriptures with a Bible teacher by your side. Each book is designed to fit in your jacket pocket or handbag so you can read it anywhere – over the breakfast table, on the commute into work or college, while you are waiting in your car, during your lunch break or in bed at night. Wherever life's journey takes you, time in God's Word is vital nourishment for your spiritual journey.

Our prayer is that these devotionals become your daily feast, a precious opportunity to meet with God through his Word. Read, meditate, apply and pray through the Scriptures given for each day, and allow God's truths to take root and transform your life.

If these devotionals whet your appetite for more, there is a 'For further study' section at the end of each book. You can also visit our website at <www.keswickministries.org/resources> to find the full range of books, study guides, CDs, DVDs and mp3s available. Why not order an audio recording of the Bible Reading series to accompany your daily devotional?

Let the word of Christ dwell in you richly.
(Colossians 3:16, ESV)

Introduction
Hebrews

Sometimes we don't see what is right in front of our eyes.

Somehow we miss the obvious, fundamental truths staring us in the face.

Many of the Jewish people in the first century certainly did.

When God called Abraham he promised to make him into a great nation and bless the whole world through his 'seed', his descendant, Christ. Abraham's descendants, the Hebrew people, were God's chosen people. But this promise – not just to set them apart as a distinct people but, through them, to bless the world – was fulfilled in the coming of a Messiah. The whole of Old Testament history, from Abraham on, orientates around the fact that one day the Messiah would step into history. But when the Messiah actually came, no-one recognized him. 'He came to that which was his own, but his own did not receive him' (John 1:11).

This letter to the Hebrews, by an unknown author, was written to address some of the fundamental misunderstandings the Jewish people had about Jesus. The author was writing to correct their ignorance of who Christ was and to explain how he completes and fulfils Israel's history, law, ceremonial rituals and priesthood.

We too can have a misconstrued understanding of Jesus and his work. So the writer to the Hebrews helps us focus our attention on the supremacy of Christ in divine revelation and the sufficiency of Christ in Christian experience. Jesus is not just a contributor to divine revelation. He *is* the divine revelation; he is the ultimate and final expression of truth. Neither does he play a passive role in our Christian lives. He is not just an onlooker or a spectator; he is the central participant.

We must not relegate him to being the patron of our systematic theology, whereby we do things in his name but have become detached from him. We can't view him merely as a teacher or an example to follow. As we explore sections of the book of Hebrews we will find that Jesus' role is so much fuller and so much more active.

Will you 'fix your thoughts . . . [and] fix your eyes on Jesus' and, along with the first readers, discover how glorious Christ really is?

Day 1

Read Hebrews 1:1–14
Key verses: Hebrews 1:1–2

....

¹In the past God spoke to our ancestors through the prophets at many times and in various ways, ²but in these last days he has spoken to us by his Son, whom he appointed heir of all things, and through whom also he made the universe.

God speaks.

The writer to the Hebrews takes this fact for granted. But it is a breathtaking truth. Contrary to all the other gods people have worshipped down through the ages, we have a God who speaks to us.

God has always spoken. The very first introduction we have to God in Genesis 1 is of a God who speaks. Ten times in Genesis 1 the Hebrew can be translated 'and God said': 'And God said, "Let there be light"' (verse 3); 'And God said, "Let there be a vault between the waters"' (verse 6). If God speaks, it follows that he has something to say that lies outside the realm of human knowledge.

Psalm 19 tells us about the natural revelation of God. Verses 1–4 say:

> The heavens declare the glory of God;
>> the skies proclaim the work of his hands.
> Day after day they pour forth speech;
>> night after night they reveal knowledge.
> They have no speech, they use no words;
>> no sound is heard from them.
> Yet their voice goes out into all the earth,
>> their words to the ends of the world.

The psalmist tells us that God speaks every night when the stars come out. Look across the vastness of the universe and see God speaking about his greatness and power. Every time a money spider runs across your desk God is telling you about his attention to detail and his interest in the smallest things.

Over the next few days we will look at the other, more specific ways God speaks to us. But today pause and appreciate God's general revelation.

Creation is God speaking to you.

Look around you. Whether you live in the inner city, the suburbs or the country, take time to appreciate God's creation. In the vastness of the sea, the snow-capped mountains, the star-filled sky, the intricacies of a spider's web, the colours of a flower petal and moss growing over stones, God speaks. What is he saying? How do these truths help you in the circumstances of your life today?

Use the following verses to praise God for how he reveals himself through creation.

Who shut up the sea behind doors
    when it burst forth from the womb . . .
when I said, 'This far you may come and no farther;
    here is where your proud waves halt'?
Have you ever given orders to the morning,
    or shown the dawn its place?
(Job 38:8, 11–12)

For in him [Christ] all things were created: things in heaven and on earth, visible and invisible, whether thrones or powers or rulers or authorities; all things have been created through him and for him. He is before all things, and in him all things hold together.
(Colossians 1:16–17)

Day 2

Read Hebrews 1:1–14; 3:1–6
Key verses: Hebrews 1:1–2, 4, 14; 3:2, 5

....

^{1}*In the past God spoke to our ancestors through the prophets at many times and in various ways,* ^{2}*but in these last days he has spoken to us by his Son . . .* ^{4}*He became as much superior to the angels as the name he has inherited is superior to theirs . . .*

^{14}*Are not all angels ministering spirits sent to serve those who will inherit salvation? . . .*

$^{3:2}$*He [Jesus] was faithful to the one who appointed him, just as . . .* ^{5}*'Moses was faithful as a servant in all God's house,' bearing witness to what would be spoken by God in the future.*

In what other ways does God speak?

The writer to the Hebrews explains the four key means by which God has spoken in the past.

• Prophets

The role of a prophet was to listen to God and to speak his words (Jeremiah 23:22). Prophets communicated God's message through preaching, often prefacing their message with 'Thus says the Lord'. They used poetry and song. Isaiah 5, for example, is the song of a vineyard. Prophets spoke through drama (Ezekiel once had to eat a scroll!) and personal experience. Hosea was told to marry a prostitute called Gomer. Her unfaithfulness mirrored Israel's unfaithfulness to God. Hosea's broken heart was a pale reflection of God's hurt.

• Priests

The priesthood is implied in Hebrews 1:3 and is developed more fully in chapters 5–10. The role of the priest was to offer sacrifices on behalf of the people. This ritual purification ceremony performed by the priests spoke of God's holiness, our sinfulness and the extreme lengths required to satisfy the just wrath of God against sin.

• Angels

The word 'angel' is often translated 'messenger'. Angels are waiting for God to give them instructions to carry messages. Seventeen times in the Old Testament and on seven occasions in the New Testament angels visited people, and each time the message they brought was binding (2:2–3).

• Moses

Exodus 33:11 says, 'The Lᴏʀᴅ would speak to Moses face to face, as one speaks to a friend.' Moses is given special mention here because of his unique place in the revelation God gave to the Hebrew people. God revealed his law to Moses and it became the plumb line, the chief legal authority, in the history of Israel.

God speaks. Are you listening?

We wish we could hear God's audible voice. The problem may not be God speaking, but our listening. God spoke in the past and still speaks today: 'So, as the Holy Spirit says: "*Today*, if you hear his voice . . ."' (Hebrews 3:7, italics added). The Bible is God's Word to us (2 Timothy 3:16; 2 Peter 1:21). Pray that you would be attentive to God's voice; be expectant that he has something to say to you. As you read Scripture ask the Holy Spirit to reveal God to you and help you obey all that he tells you to do. Keep this daily time with God a high priority.

Bible Matters by Tim Chester (IVP, 2017) is a helpful book on this subject if you would like to read further.

Day 3

Read Hebrews 1:1–14; 2:5–9; 3:1–6
Key verses: Hebrews 1:1–2

. . . .

¹In the past God spoke to our ancestors through the prophets at many times and in various ways, ²but in these last days he has spoken to us by his Son, whom he appointed heir of all things, and through whom also he made the universe.

God saved the best till last.

Look at verses 1–2 again. Jesus is God's final Word, because in him is the fullness of God's revelation.

He was superior to the priests. They had to offer sacrifices continually for their own sin and the sins of the people (Hebrews 7:27). But Jesus is seated in heaven now because no more sacrifices are needed (Hebrews 1:3). His death was a one-off event, sufficient to pay the penalty for sin in full.

Hebrews 1:5–8 explains why Jesus is also superior to the angels. God never spoke to angels the way he spoke to his Son. When he became a man Jesus was made lower than the angels, but now he is back in his rightful place, 'crowned with glory and honour' (2:9).

Jesus is superior to the prophets, priests, angels and Moses, not because he was a better preacher, had a better message or was more trustworthy. Their message was true and they were all bearing witness to the truth. But Jesus is supreme because he is himself the truth (John 14:6). He himself is the message and therefore has unmatched supremacy in God's revelation.

This letter to the Hebrews was written to a group of people so wrapped up in all the true things God had revealed through his agents in the past that they had missed the fulfilment to which it all pointed: Christ.

Don't make the same mistake. Don't study the Bible to acquire knowledge or rules for life (John 5:39–40). Look for Christ in the Scriptures. Meet him there.

Jesus is the truth and his teaching was shamelessly centred on himself. Meditate on the following words of Jesus. Let them encourage and equip you for the day ahead.

I am the bread of life. Whoever comes to me will never go hungry, and whoever believes in me will never be thirsty.
(John 6:35)

I am the light of the world. Whoever follows me will never walk in darkness, but will have the light of life.
(John 8:12)

I am the gate; whoever enters through me will be saved . . . I have come that they may have life, and have it to the full.
(John 10:9–10)

I am the good shepherd. The good shepherd lays down his life for the sheep.
(John 10:11)

I am the resurrection and the life. The one who believes in me will live, even though they die.
(John 11:25)

I am the way and the truth and the life. No one comes to the Father except through me.
(John 14:6)

I am the vine; you are the branches. If you remain in me and I in you, you will bear much fruit; apart from me you can do nothing.
(John 15:5)

Day 4

Read Hebrews 1:1–3; 2:1–18

Key verse: Hebrews 1:3

· ·

³The Son is the radiance of God's glory and the exact representation of his being, sustaining all things by his powerful word.

'What is truth?' asked Pilate, the Roman governor (John 18:38).

That is a universal question most people ask at some point. Is there such a thing as truth?

Today it is unpopular to talk about absolute truth. Truth is whatever works for you. Your opinions and assertions are just as valid as mine. But Jesus went beyond that to claiming to be the truth. He claimed to be the truth about:

• God

  If you want to know what God is like, look at Jesus. Everything Jesus is, God is. Paul says in 2 Timothy 1:12,

'I know *whom* I have believed' (italics added). He does not say, 'I know *what* I have believed.' Knowing what you believe is important, but Christianity is about knowing someone, not something! We can learn facts about God, such as that he is omniscient (all-knowing), omnipotent (all-powerful), omnipresent (in all places), eternal and immutable (unchanging), but these truths won't establish a relationship and provoke us to love him. The more we know, love and trust Jesus, the more we will know, love and trust God. In fact, it is only when we know Christ that we know God.

• Humanity

Hebrews 1:3 is speaking not just about Jesus' deity but also his humanity. Human beings were created in God's image, to portray the truth about him (Genesis 1:27). That means that if you looked at Adam you would see the visible, physical portrayal of the invisible, spiritual God. Adam would be kind because God was kind. The way Adam treated Eve, the way they looked after the animals and tended the garden, showed what God was like. But together they sinned and God's image was tarnished. Their life and behaviour no longer showed what God was like. Jesus came as the 'second man', the 'last Adam'. He is the radiance of God's glory, the truth about God that humanity was intended to express.

We were created, and are now redeemed, to portray a physical and visible expression of the moral character of God, of which Jesus was the prototype.

Schools, the government, magazines and the media inform our thinking about what it means to be human. They shape our moral character by subtly, in a myriad different ways, influencing our values, priorities and attitudes.

Select and read an account from one of the Gospels. What do you learn in the character of Jesus about the character of God? How is this to be your character too?

Today, Jesus is our life and his character is to be expressed in every task, conversation and encounter. Ask the Holy Spirit to live the character of Christ in you. As King David prayed:

Show me your ways, LORD,
    teach me your paths.
Guide me in your truth and teach me,
    for you are God my Saviour,
    and my hope is in you all day long.
(Psalm 25:4–5)

Day 5

Read Hebrews 2:1–18
Key verses: Hebrews 2:10–11

....

> [10] *In bringing many sons and daughters to glory, it was fitting that God, for whom and through whom everything exists, should make the pioneer of their salvation perfect through what he suffered.* [11] *Both the one who makes people holy and those who are made holy are of the same family. So Jesus is not ashamed to call them brothers and sisters.*

We talk of 'going to glory' when we die, meaning we are going to heaven. But that's not how the Bible uses the term 'glory'. When the Bible speaks of glory, it refers to the character of God.

John says of Jesus, 'The Word became flesh and made his dwelling among us. We have seen his glory, the glory of the one and only Son, who came from the Father, full of grace and truth' (John 1:14). In Jesus we see what God is like: we see the character of God; we see the glory of God.

Sin is the extent to which we 'fall short of the glory of God' (Romans 3:23). Sin is not so much a measurement of how bad we are, but of how good we are not! We have come short. We don't show what God is like any more. We've become selfish and live for our own agendas. Now, in Jesus, we see the glory of God fully expressed – but more than that, we see one whose goal it is to 'bring many sons and daughters to glory'. Restoring what was lost in the fall, restoring God's glory to human experience, was the object of Jesus' work and ministry.

That's why Colossians 1:27 says, 'Christ in you, the hope of glory.' Jesus brings us back to glory, the glory we have sinned against and come short of. The Scriptures are true, but it is Christ who is the truth; Christ who by his indwelling presence in your life makes this journey real. It was foreshadowed in the time of the prophets, but now in Christ we see how he equips us to be what God intended human beings to be.

Think: you are God's image-bearer.

Yes, sin has tarnished that image, but even now Jesus is restoring us to glory in a continuing process. 'We all, who with unveiled faces contemplate the Lord's glory, are being transformed into his image with ever-increasing glory, which comes from the Lord, who is the

Spirit' (2 Corinthians 3:18). One day, when Jesus returns, we will fully and finally be like him (Philippians 1:6).

Until then, join God in his work.

'Contemplate the Lord's glory' by:

- keeping your focus on Jesus (Hebrews 12:2);
- adopting his attitudes (Philippians 2:5);
- studying and meditating on his Word (John 17:17);
- allowing God's Word to renew your mind and thoughts (Romans 12:2).

Take an honest look at your tarnished image of God. In what specific ways does Christ need to be more evident within you? Pray that the Holy Spirit would continue his process of transformation so that you might represent God well to all the people you meet today.

Day 6

Read Hebrews 3:7–19
Key verses: Hebrews 3:7–11

....

7 So, as the Holy Spirit says:
'Today, if you hear his voice,
 8 do not harden your hearts
as you did in the rebellion,
 during the time of testing in the wilderness,
9 where your ancestors tested and tried me,
 though for forty years they saw what I did.
10 That is why I was angry with that generation;
 I said, "Their hearts are always going astray,
and they have not known my ways."
11 So I declared on oath in my anger,
 "They shall never enter my rest." '

A picture speaks a thousand words.

Here we have a graphic description of the exodus to press home the first of five stark warnings that occur in this epistle. Jewish Christians would have known the story well. It was the most glorious event in Israel's history, when God intervened and delivered them from years of slavery. But it was also one of the most disastrous events in their history. They spent forty years in a wilderness, going nowhere and doing nothing.

The writer retells this story because it is full of typology, pictures, pointing to Christ and our Christian life. Egypt is portrayed as slavery to sin, as we read in the book of Jude. The Passover lamb is a picture of Christ (John 1:29). The exodus itself depicts deliverance from sin. In fact, at the transfiguration Jesus' death is called his exodus (Luke 9:31). Crossing the Red Sea is a picture of baptism, of death to the old life and resurrection to the new (1 Corinthians 10:2). Canaan is portrayed in Hebrews 4 as resting in Christ and enjoying the fullness of his presence in our lives.

The problem was that the first generation of Israelites leaving Egypt never got to Canaan. The journey that should have taken only eleven days (Deuteronomy 1:2) took them forty years! The writer's point is that they were saved from slavery in Egypt but did not enter into the fullness of God's purposes for them, and instead got stuck going round in circles because they weren't listening to God.

The same can happen to us. We stop listening to God and, although we are saved, we make little or no progress in our Christian lives. Saved but stuck!

Are you saved but stuck?

'The preaching isn't inspiring.' 'I'm too busy to read my Bible.' 'My spouse doesn't encourage me.' We can come up with a host of excuses for why we're spiritually stuck in a rut. But sometimes we've got to face up to the fact that we are distant from God because we choose to be. It is our responsibility. Instead of listening to, obeying and trusting God, we ignore him.

As the Holy Spirit speaks to you today, respond to God's love, mercy and grace with obedience.

Pray with the psalmist:

GOD, teach me lessons for living
    so I can stay the course.
Give me insight so I can do what you tell me –
    my whole life one long, obedient response . . .
Give me a bent for your words of wisdom,
    and not for piling up loot.
Divert my eyes from toys and trinkets,
    invigorate me on the pilgrim way . . .

See how hungry I am for your counsel;
  preserve my life through your righteous ways!
(Psalm 119:33–40, MSG)

Day 7

Read Hebrews 3:7–19
Key verses: Hebrews 3:16–19

....

> ¹⁶*Who were they who heard and rebelled? Were they not all those Moses led out of Egypt?* ¹⁷*And with whom was he angry for forty years? Was it not with those who sinned, whose bodies perished in the wilderness?* ¹⁸*And to whom did God swear that they would never enter his rest if not to those who disobeyed?* ¹⁹*So we see that they were not able to enter, because of their unbelief.*

When the Israelites crossed the Red Sea God didn't wipe his brow and say, 'Phew, they're out! That's it – mission accomplished!'

Leaving Egypt was not the goal. God rescued the Israelites from Egypt so that they could come into Canaan and, from there, bless the world. God had made his purpose clear when he called Moses at the burning bush: 'I have come down to rescue them from the hand of the

Egyptians and to bring them up out of that land into a good and spacious land, a land flowing with milk and honey' (Exodus 3:8).

God's plan that he revealed to Moses wasn't anything new. He was keeping his promise to Abraham and re-establishing the original purpose for which he had set Israel apart. Many times in the wilderness he reminded the Israelites of this purpose: 'I am the LORD your God, who brought you out of Egypt to give you the land of Canaan and to be your God' (Leviticus 25:38; also Deuteronomy 6:23).

Why did God save you? To ease your guilty conscience? So you might be forgiven? So you could go to heaven instead of hell? These are wonderful aspects of the gospel. But in the New Testament, in the preaching of Jesus, in the preaching of the apostles (and we have nineteen messages or fragments of messages in the book of Acts: eight by Peter, nine by Paul, one by Stephen and one by Philip), going to heaven is never once given as the reason for becoming a Christian. That is a consequence, but it's never the reason.

So what is the reason?

The reason is that we might be reconciled to God and live in fellowship and union with him. Paul summed up

God's desire for us: 'that you may be filled to the measure of all the fullness of God' (Ephesians 3:19). The goal of the Christian life is not to get us out of hell and into heaven but to get God out of heaven and into us.

When you became a Christian, God did not wipe his brow and say, 'Phew, that's it! He/she is saved!' He had much grander plans, much larger ambitions, for you. Don't be satisfied with a rescue ticket to heaven. Live the life God intended for you now in the power he provides. Press on to Christian maturity (see what this looks like in Ephesians 4) and be filled with all the fullness of God.

Pray Paul's prayer for yourself:

> I pray that out of his glorious riches he may strengthen you with power through his Spirit in your inner being, so that Christ may dwell in your hearts through faith. And I pray that you, being rooted and established in love, may have power, together with all the Lord's holy people, to grasp how wide and long and high and deep is the love of Christ, and to know this love that surpasses knowledge – that you may be filled to the measure of all the fullness of God.
> (Ephesians 3:16–19)

Day 8

Read Hebrews 3:7 – 4:2
Key verses: Hebrews 4:1–2

....

> [1] *Therefore, since the promise of entering his rest still stands, let us be careful that none of you be found to have fallen short of it.* [2] *For we also have had the good news proclaimed to us, just as they did; but the message they heard was of no value to them, because they did not share the faith of those who obeyed.*

Fish and chips. Salt and vinegar. A toddler's grubby hands and newly painted walls. Some combinations work together but others . . . well, they just don't. In these verses we are presented with one combination which works and one which doesn't.

Throughout chapter 3 God has stated why the Israelites didn't get into Canaan. Verses 7–8 say:

Today, if you hear his voice,
do not harden your hearts
as you did in the rebellion.

And again in verse 10:

That is why I was angry with that generation;
I said, 'Their hearts are always going astray,
and they have not known my ways.'

Their hearts were hard, unbelieving and wayward. Hard hearts combined with faithlessness is a fatal combination (4:2). So even though the Israelites heard the good news, it didn't do them any good because they refused to combine it with faith.

God offers us a better, a winning, combination: the truth, the good news of the gospel, combined with faith.

Perhaps the good news was preached or explained to you. You may have accepted the truth and become a Christian. Your sins have been forgiven and you've received the gift of eternal life. But that was just the start. You need to keep on believing and trusting. You need to combine truth with continuing faith.

Truth in itself doesn't do us any good unless it is combined with faith. The Authorized Version talks of it being 'mixed with faith' (Hebrews 4:2, KJV). If you detach truth from faith, it is of no value.

The combination we need is truth coupled with faith.

We will look at what faith is tomorrow. But today, give yourself a spiritual health check and examine your heart. You might not describe yourself as 'hard-hearted' towards God but perhaps your devotion is compromised by being coupled with a particular sin. It could be:

- refusing to forgive someone who has hurt you;
- jealousy towards someone in church;
- spending habits that are out of control;
- a pornography habit you can't break;
- sexual activity outside marriage.

Repent before God. Pray with King David: 'Create in me a pure heart, O God, and renew a steadfast spirit within me' (Psalm 51:10).

O to grace how great a debtor
Daily I'm constrained to be!
Let thy goodness, like a fetter,
Bind my wandering heart to thee.

Prone to wander, Lord, I feel it,

Prone to leave the God I love;

Here's my heart, O take and seal it,

Seal it for thy courts above.

(Robert Robinson, 'Come Thou Fount of Every Blessing',

1757)

Day 9

Read Hebrews 3:12 – 4:2
Key verses: Hebrews 4:1–2

....

[1] Therefore, since the promise of entering his rest still stands, let us be careful that none of you be found to have fallen short of it. [2] For we also have had the good news proclaimed to us, just as they did; but the message they heard was of no value to them, because they did not share the faith of those who obeyed.

What is faith?

Is it a mystical force you conjure up if you close your eyes and really believe something strongly enough to make it happen?

Is it a leap in the dark when you've run out of facts?

No. Faith is not believing that black is white. Nor is it a substitute for facts. Indeed, faith needs facts; it needs an object. And it is the object in which you place your faith which determines the validity of it. You could have a lot of faith in thin ice but you'd still sink!

When you sit on a chair you exercise faith. What does that mean? It means you sit down, trusting the chair to take the strain. When you have faith in an aircraft it means you get on board, trusting the plane to fly through the air. So what is faith in God? It is acting in obedience and trusting God to work.

On their release from Egypt the Hebrews had ample evidence of God's utter sufficiency in his work on their behalf. But as soon as they got to Kadesh Barnea they forgot about daily dependence on him and looked only to themselves.

Twelve men were sent to explore the land God had promised them (Numbers 13:1–2). They saw the bountiful produce but were overawed by the powerful inhabitants. Ten of the spies, conscious of their own inadequacy and lack of experience in warfare, concluded, 'We can't attack those people; they are stronger than we are' (Numbers 13:31). Only Joshua and Caleb spoke up, reminding the Israelites that God was with them, working on their behalf (Numbers 14:6–9).

We too have seen God working on our behalf. We've experienced his forgiveness and his Holy Spirit within us.

But, having been saved by faith, we try to live by human effort, detached from dependence on God.

One of the features of the Christian life is that our lives become explicable only in terms of God working in us and through us. Would your marriage be different if you weren't a Christian? Would your family life be different if you weren't living in the power of the risen Christ? Would your church be different if God withdrew?

Have you become detached from dependence on God? Have you become so aware of how large the obstacles are or how great your inadequacy is that you have stopped letting God be God? Think through all the ways that God has worked on your behalf in the past. Write these blessings down and thank God for them.

Remember, you are not putting your faith in something flimsy. You are putting your faith in the creator and sustainer of the universe, who wants to work in your situation. Will you have faith today?

Day 10

Read Hebrews 4:1–11
Key verses: Hebrews 4:9–11

....

⁹There remains, then, a Sabbath-rest for the people of God; ¹⁰for anyone who enters God's rest also rests from their works, just as God did from his. ¹¹Let us, therefore, make every effort to enter that rest, so that no one will perish by following their example of disobedience.

Is it helpful to bring up the past and dwell on previous mistakes?

Sometimes.

The writer is not retelling the exodus story to discourage his readers by saying, 'Look at what the Israelites did. You are in danger of doing the same thing.' Having given them the bad news of their unbelief and failure to live by faith in God, he wants to remind them: 'the promise of entering his rest still stands' (4:1).

This word 'rest' is repeated often in these verses. What do we mean by 'rest'? More importantly, what does the Bible mean by 'rest'? The writer defines it in verses 9–10 as a Sabbath-rest. In other words, he is saying that there is a human experience that corresponds with the divine experience of God's rest.

Why did God rest at the end of creation? God's energy is inexhaustible, so he didn't rest because he was tired. He rested because he had finished. Big difference. The Sabbath-rest is a picture of God's sufficiency. The Christian calendar caught up with this principle only after the resurrection of Jesus and the gift of the Holy Spirit, and now we rest on the first day of the week, symbolically portraying the truth that we rest in the sufficiency of his risen life.

Jesus still offers rest to those who come to him in dependence, relying on his sufficiency (Matthew 11:28–30).

Affirm with the psalmist:

Yes, my soul, find rest in God;
  my hope comes from him.
Truly he is my rock and my salvation;
  he is my fortress, I shall not be shaken.
My salvation and my honour depend on God;
  he is my mighty rock, my refuge.

> Trust in him at all times, you people;
>> pour out your hearts to him,
>> for God is our refuge.
>
> (Psalm 62:5–8)

Resting means daily depending on God. In the psalmist's words, it is trusting him 'at all times' (verse 8). This is a big statement – one we continually need to be intentional about putting into practice. Is there a relationship, situation or concern you need to entrust to God today? Will you demonstrate your dependence on God's sufficiency by trusting him with it?

Day 11

Read Hebrews 4:1–11
Key verse: Hebrews 4:11

....

¹¹Let us, therefore, make every effort to enter that rest, so that no one will perish by following their example of disobedience.

Did you notice what seems like a contradiction in chapter 4?

The writer tells us to depend on God, but then says, 'Let us, therefore, make every effort to enter that rest.' Having to make an effort to enter into a place of rest certainly sounds like a contradiction!

But think for a moment.

If I asked you, 'What makes your car work?' you would say, 'The engine.' The engine is the power that takes the car down the road. Without the engine the car is good for nothing. Jesus Christ, by his indwelling Holy Spirit, is the power that enables us to live the Christian life. As he said, 'apart from me you can do nothing' (John 15:5).

But right now your car has an engine under the bonnet doing nothing. Why? Because it needs a driver to put it in gear and steer it down the road. What makes the car go? Is it the engine? Is it the driver? It is both!

What makes the Christian life work? Is it Christ? Is it me? It is both: we're workers together with God. Of course, Christ, like the engine, is the indispensable part: he works in us to will and to act according to his good purpose (Philippians 2:13). He works in us to motivate, direct and channel us. But you and I have to learn to become the driver, to exercise those disciplines that keep us in touch with God. The driver's job is to enable the power of the engine to make contact with the wheels so that the car is empowered to go down the road. Our responsibility is to enable God's indwelling power to make contact with our life as we bring him into every situation and circumstance.

Obedience to God and dependence on him cannot be separated. Obedience without dependence will lead to legalism. Dependence without obedience will lead to unhealthy mysticism. But obedience coupled with dependence on him for the resources we need will lead to dynamism.

'There remains,' says the writer, 'a rest for the people of God.' God is inviting you to live in the richness of everything that's intended for you. God calls this 'entering into rest'. There will be nothing you face in your life that is bigger than the resources you have in the Lord Jesus Christ.

But you will never prove it until you trust and obey.

Would you like to experience more of the power of God? The key is obedience and trust together. Throughout the history of Israel every act of God was precipitated by an act of obedience. Think about Joshua leading the people across the River Jordan. It was only as the priests placed their feet in the water, in obedient response to and dependence on God, that God parted the waves before them (Joshua 3). The principle still operates. What obedience does God require from you today? As the provocative title of John Ortberg's book states, 'If you want to walk on water, you've got to get out of the boat' (Zondervan, 2001).

Day 12

Read Hebrews 4:14 – 5:10

Key verses: Hebrews 5:1–4

∙∙

[1] Every high priest is selected from among the people and is appointed to represent the people in matters related to God, to offer gifts and sacrifices for sins. [2] He is able to deal gently with those who are ignorant and are going astray, since he himself is subject to weakness. [3] This is why he has to offer sacrifices for his own sins, as well as for the sins of the people. [4] And no one takes this honour upon himself, but he receives it when called by God, just as Aaron was.

What image does the word 'priest' bring to mind? Flowing robes, confessional booths, salacious newspaper headlines?

'Priest' is not a popular word in the Protestant vocabulary, particularly in nonconformist circles. Indeed, the word never appears in the letters of Paul, Peter, James or Jude, nor in the writings of John. This is the only epistle in which the word 'priest' occurs, and it occurs twenty-eight times:

in every chapter from 2 to 10, and then as the writer sums up at the end of chapter 13.

Hebrews 5:1 explains that a priest is an intermediary who stands between two parties and connects them with each other. The priest stood between God and humanity for the purpose of bringing them together and reconnecting them. And in the book of Hebrews the emphasis is on the priesthood of Christ. In fact, twenty-four of the twenty-eight references to priest have to do with the priesthood of Christ.

The Jews reading this letter would have been able to understand Jesus' priesthood because they were familiar with the Levitical priesthood – what the book of Hebrews calls the Aaronic priesthood. From the tribe of Levi, Moses' brother, Aaron, and his family line were chosen to be priests (Exodus 28:1). So, when Aaron died, his son, Eleazar, replaced him. And before the Israelites entered Canaan the Lord set apart the whole tribe of Levi, of which Moses and Aaron were members, to serve as priests (Deuteronomy 10:6–9). The function of the priests was right at the very core of their worship. If the priests didn't turn up, worship shut down.

We too need a priest. Someone to bridge the gap between us and a holy God. Someone to represent us before God. Someone to act as an intermediary.

Jesus is our great high priest. He connects us to God and pleads our case when we sin. He prayed for us in John 17 and is still interceding for us before God the Father.

> Therefore he is able to save completely those who come to God through him, because he always lives to intercede for them.
> (Hebrews 7:25)

> Who will bring any charge against those whom God has chosen? It is God who justifies. Who then is the one who condemns? No one. Christ Jesus who died – more than that, who was raised to life – is at the right hand of God and is also interceding for us.
> (Romans 8:33–34)

We confess our sins to Christ, our high priest, grateful that his death was sufficient to pay the price for our sins. His intercessory role as our priest connects us with the Father. Think of the sins you have already committed today – the secret sins and the persistent ones. Repent and take strength from knowing that Jesus is praying for you. He is bringing your name before the Father.

Day 13

Read Hebrews 7:1–28
Key verses: Hebrews 7:11, 16–17

....

[11] If perfection could have been attained through the Levitical priesthood . . . why was there still need for another priest to come, one in the order of Melchizedek, not in the order of Aaron? . . . [16] [Jesus] has become a priest not on the basis of a regulation as to his ancestry but on the basis of the power of an indestructible life. [17] For it is declared:

> *'You are a priest for ever,*
> > *in the order of Melchizedek.'*

The writer to the Hebrews had a problem. The priests in the line of Aaron did not accurately or adequately fore-shadow the priesthood of Christ.

Jesus was not a Levite and therefore was not qualified to serve as a priest (7:14). The Aaronic priests were subject to weakness (5:2) – they had to deal with their own sin before addressing the sins of the people (7:27); they could offer sacrifices for the forgiveness of sin but not clear the conscience of the worshipper (9:9); and they had to repeat the sacrifice again and again – their work was never finished (10:11).

So the author rummages around in Old Testament history and finds an obscure man, Melchizedek, mentioned briefly in Genesis 14:18–20 and referred to in Psalm 110:4.

Melchizedek could represent Christ because of some key similarities:

• He had no genealogy (7:3).

   The Aaronic priesthood was based entirely on genealogy. You couldn't be a priest if you couldn't trace your ancestry back to Aaron (Ezra 2:62). But just as no mention is made of Melchizedek's genealogy, Jesus had no father and mother in his ultimate origin (John 1:1–2).

• He lasts for ever (7:3).

   'Without beginning of days or end of life, resembling the Son of God, he remains a priest for ever.' Again, this is arguing from the silence of Scripture, which mentions nothing of Melchizedek's death.

- He was king of righteousness and being king of Salem meant he was king of peace (7:2).

  These themes of righteousness and kingship correspond to Christ, as the writer explains in 1:8:

  > But about the Son he says,
  >> 'Your throne, O God, will last for ever and ever;
  >>> a sceptre of justice will be the sceptre of your
  >>>> kingdom.'

- He elicits the same response (7:4).

When Abraham returned from a victorious battle he gave Melchizedek 10% of everything he possessed. Whereas the Levitical priest collected a tenth from the people, Abraham had no obligation to pay Melchizedek: he gave it voluntarily. In the same way, our response to Jesus is voluntary. The Holy Spirit is involved in our coming to Christ, but we are not forced to come: the way is open to us to come voluntarily.

What a great high priest we have! He ministers in 'the power of an indestructible life' so is able to save completely and for all time. Worship him today.

Before the throne of God above
I have a strong, a perfect plea;

A great High Priest, whose name is Love,
Who ever lives and pleads for me.
My name is graven on his hands,
My name is written on his heart;
I know that while in heaven he stands
No tongue can bid me thence depart.
(Charitie Lees Bancroft, 'Before the Throne
of God Above', 1863)

Day 14

Read Hebrews 7:1–28

Key verses: Hebrews 7:26–28

....

> [26] *Such a high priest truly meets our need – one who is holy, blameless, pure, set apart from sinners, exalted above the heavens.* [27] *Unlike the other high priests, he does not need to offer sacrifices day after day, first for his own sins, and then for the sins of the people. He sacrificed for their sins once for all when he offered himself.* [28] *For the law appoints as high priests men in all their weakness; but the oath, which came after the law, appointed the Son, who has been made perfect for ever.*

'It is finished.'

Jesus' cry from the cross signalled that no more blood need ever be shed for sin. The temple curtain, the barrier that separated the Most Holy Place from the people and which could be approached only by a priest with blood on the Day of Atonement, was torn, not as a human act from bottom to top, but as a divine act from top to bottom. From that moment every priest in Israel was out of a job.

Jesus offered himself once and for all, and then he sat down (8:1).

The writer to the Hebrews states that this qualifies Jesus to be our priest and mediator. The grounds of our access to God and our accessibility to God are not based on our personal credentials, any more than they were based on the personal credentials of the Israelites. They could approach God only because of the credentials of the priest. And we have a priest who is totally adequate: who you are, what your history is, what your background is, what sins you are up to your neck in – all this is irrelevant to the sufficiency of Christ to serve as our priest. We can approach God through Christ our priest, because it's the priest who is acceptable to God; it's the priest who addresses God and reconciles us.

That's why it says in Hebrews 4:14–16:

> Since we have a great high priest who has ascended into heaven, Jesus the Son of God, let us hold firmly to the faith we profess. For we do not have a high priest who is unable to feel sympathy for our weaknesses, but we have one who has been tempted in every way, just as we are –

yet he did not sin. Let us then approach God's throne of grace with confidence, so that we may receive mercy and find grace to help us in our time of need.

Jesus is your perfect high priest. So, today:

• hold firmly to the faith you profess (Hebrews 4:14);
• receive mercy and grace in your time of need (4:16);
• draw near to God (7:19);
• be assured of your salvation (7:25);
• serve God without guilt (9:14);
• look forward to your eternal inheritance (9:15);
• accept that you have been made holy (10:10).

Today, talk to your priest, the Lord Jesus Christ. Confess your sins and thank him for his strength and help as you bring your needs before him.

Day 15

Read Hebrews 8:1–13
Key verse: Hebrews 8:10

· ·

> ¹⁰*This is the covenant I will establish with the*
> *people of Israel*
> *after that time, declares the Lord.*
> *I will put my laws in their minds*
> *and write them on their hearts.*
> *I will be their God,*
> *and they will be my people.*

What had gone wrong?

Hebrews 8:7–12 is a direct quotation from Jeremiah 31 containing a prophetic announcement and definition of a new covenant God promised he would bring to the house of Israel. Clearly there was something wrong with the first covenant or it wouldn't have needed to be replaced (verse 7).

The two covenants are concerned with the same law, so there was nothing wrong with the law itself. Indeed, the law is unchangeable because it is a revelation of the moral character of God, which is immutable, unchanging. For example, when the law says, 'You shall not commit adultery', it is because God is totally faithful and this is an expression of his character. That's why Jesus said, in the Sermon on the Mount, that 'until heaven and earth disappear, not the smallest letter, not the least stroke of a pen, will by any means disappear from the Law until everything is accomplished' (Matthew 5:18). God doesn't change, doesn't wind down, doesn't grow up, and doesn't get better. So the law, which expresses his character, is as unchangeable as he is.

There was nothing wrong with the law itself; the failure was in the people's ability to keep it. Moses had come down the mountain with the law of God, and the people agreed to obey it. They repeated their declaration in the book of Deuteronomy, and they said it again in the book of Joshua and at various other intervals. But they couldn't keep their promise. Of course they couldn't!

The fundamental difference between the two covenants is that under the old covenant, the onus was on the people. They had to keep the Ten Commandments. 'You shall have no other gods before me.' 'You shall not make for yourself an image.' 'You, you, you . . .' In contrast, under the new covenant, the onus is on God. God said, 'I will put my laws in their minds and write them on their hearts. I will be their God . . . I will forgive their wickedness.'

The first covenant was 'You do it'; in the new covenant God said, 'I will do it.'

Today, rest in the freedom and joy of knowing that your salvation and the security of your covenant relationship with God are not dependent on you. They are based solely on Christ's work on the cross and his resurrection life in you. So, if you are:

- aware of your failure and inability,
- frustrated with your own sense of inadequacy,
- discouraged by events within and around you,

. . . remember, it is Christ's relentless working in you that is the basis for your relationship with God and your fruitfulness. It is Christ's performance that counts, not yours.

Day 16

Read Hebrews 8:1–13; 10:8–18
Key verse: Hebrews 8:10

....

> [10] *This is the covenant I will establish with the*
>   *people of Israel*
>   *after that time, declares the Lord.*
> *I will put my laws in their minds*
>   *and write them on their hearts.*
> *I will be their God,*
>   *and they will be my people.*

Have you ever house-trained a dog or a cat?

You reward good behaviour and discipline bad behaviour. If you do it well, they may behave perfectly – but only as long as you are there! Their modified behaviour is on the basis of reward for the good and punishment for the bad; there is no moral consciousness involved.

All the law can ever do is house-train us. Written on tablets of stone, it was external. It could demand righteousness but never accomplish it. At best, it might house-train us by its offer of reward or punishment. How do you know if you've been house-trained? Check how you live when nobody is looking. If you live one way when people are looking and another way when they're not, you haven't been sanctified – you've just been house-trained!

The new covenant changes all this. No longer is the law imposed from the outside; it is placed inside us by the indwelling power of the Holy Spirit. The same law, once written on stone, is now written on our hearts and minds. The new covenant doesn't revise the law; it simply relocates it.

And as well as having a new priest ministering for us, there is also a new power operating in us: the indwelling presence of the Spirit of Jesus Christ.

The Holy Spirit implements this new covenant (Ezekiel 36:27; John 14:17). What were commands under the old covenant actually become promises under the new (Romans 8:3–4). So when the law says, 'You shall not steal', you don't. Why? Because you are more disciplined than you used to be? No. It's because the Spirit of God is in you; he gives you a hunger and a thirst for righteousness, and he works in you to will and to do his good pleasure. This righteousness doesn't work from the outside in, by our trying to keep the law and do better. It's a righteousness that is released from the inside out as the Spirit of God writes the law of God in our hearts. That's why righteousness in the New Testament is described as fruit (Philippians 1:11). Fruit is a consequence of life; and the fruit of righteousness flows out naturally because the Spirit of God is in us.

Thank God for every evidence of the Spirit's work in your life – every decision, action, thought, conversation that was God-directed and God-initiated. Thank the Holy Spirit that it is his business to write God's law in even larger letters on our hearts as an expression of his righteous character.

Daily rely on the Holy Spirit's resources.

- If you are facing sexual temptation, draw on the Spirit's help to do what the law commands: 'You shall not commit adultery' (Exodus 20:14).
- If you struggle with greed, draw on the Spirit's help to do what the law commands: 'You shall not covet' (Exodus 20:17).
- If you are struggling to get your priorities right, draw on the Spirit's help to do what the law commands: 'You shall have no other gods before me' (Exodus 20:3).

Day 17

Read Hebrews 8:10–12; 9:11 – 10:25

Key verses: Hebrews 8:10–11

. . . .

*¹⁰ This is the covenant I will establish with the
    people of Israel
  after that time, declares the Lord.
I will put my laws in their minds
  and write them on their hearts.
I will be their God,
  and they will be my people.
¹¹ No longer will they teach their neighbours,
  or say to one another, 'Know the Lord,'
because they will all know me,
  from the least of them to the greatest.*

Teachers, business colleagues, church ministers, spouses, friends. We have a variety of people in our lives, but who do we have a deep relationship with? It is those individuals we *know*, not just *know about*.

God said the new covenant would produce a new relationship. People would no longer be taught about the Lord; instead, 'they will all know me' (Jeremiah 31:34). There would be a new intimacy. The law would be in their hearts.

In 2 Peter 1:3 it says, 'His divine power has given us everything we need for a godly life through our knowledge of him who called us by his own glory and goodness.'

And 2 Peter 3:18 says, 'Grow in the grace and knowledge of our Lord and Saviour Jesus Christ.'

That's why we spend time in our Bibles: not to get to know the Bible but to get to know Christ, who is revealed through the Scriptures. The living Word is revealed through the written Word.

The least of us to the greatest will know God. That's an interesting progression. Knowledge of God is not obtained. It's received; it's dependent on revelation. As Jesus said in Matthew 11:25–26, 'I praise you, Father, Lord of heaven and earth, because you have hidden these things from the wise and learned, and revealed them to little children. Yes, Father, for this is what you were pleased to do.' That's why we come in humility, as children, and say, 'Lord, reveal more of yourself.'

And out of this new relationship – knowing God, knowing *whom* we have believed – comes a new righteousness (2 Timothy 1:12). The more you know Christ, the more you become like him. It's a process: we're being transformed from one degree of glory to another, in his image.

Don't think of reading your Bible as another chore to get through, another item to tick off the 'to do' list. See it for what it is: an opportunity to encounter Christ and become more like him. As the apostle Paul reminds us:

> And we all, who with unveiled faces contemplate the Lord's glory, are being transformed into his image with ever-increasing glory, which comes from the Lord, who is the Spirit.
> (2 Corinthians 3:18)

Jesus is the Father's glory (John 1:14). Today, contemplate him. Reread Hebrews 8 – 10 about Jesus, our great high priest. Meet him in the Scriptures. Ask the Holy Spirit to reveal Christ to you in a fresh way and to transform you into his likeness.

Day 18

Read Hebrews 8:10–12; 9:11–15; 10:1–25
Key verses: Hebrews 8:12; 9:13–14

. . . .

> [12]*For I will forgive their wickedness*
> *and will remember their sins no more . . .*
> [9:13]*The blood of goats and bulls and the ashes of a heifer sprinkled on those who are ceremonially unclean sanctify them so that they are outwardly clean.* [14]*How much more, then, will the blood of Christ, who through the eternal Spirit offered himself unblemished to God, cleanse our consciences from acts that lead to death, so that we may serve the living God!*

Remember the days when everyone had a chequebook?

The paper a cheque is written on is intrinsically worthless; it is valid only for as much cash as there is in the bank. However, if you've no cash in the bank you can postdate a cheque to the end of the month when you get your salary. You write the postdated cheque and the debt is covered, but it's not removed.

The blood of bulls and goats was like a cheque; worthless in itself, it covered sin but did not remove it (Hebrews 10:11). But when Jesus, on the cross, cried, 'It is finished', he was saying: 'There's cash in the bank! The cheque is now valid!' And all the Old Testament believers cashed their cheques.

Now we're dealing with the real currency, not the postdated cheque. The real currency is not the blood of bulls and goats but the precious blood of Christ. This currency doesn't just cover sin; it removes sin, to the extent that the Father says, 'I will remember their sins no more.' This doesn't mean that God is forgetful. It means he never recalls your sin; he never brings it up again. This promise has nothing to do with what we deserve, but everything to do with the quality of our priest.

Jesus is both the sacrifice and the priest. He didn't merely offer sacrifices, he was the sacrifice, and it's by his blood that we, with confidence, have access to God. The whole saving work of Christ is encompassed in this new covenant. Our sins are forgiven at the cross. Having been forgiven, we come to the empty tomb so that we might get to know the living Christ and the power of his resurrection.

And from there we go to Pentecost, where God says, 'I'll put my Spirit in you, and I'll move you to follow my decrees and keep my law.'

This is the new covenant. Are you living in the good of it?

If you've confessed your sin to God, don't keep dwelling on it and wallowing in guilt. Believe the Father's promise, 'I will remember your sins no more'. You are forgiven by the precious blood of Christ. Savour this truth and serve in the joy of it.

When Satan tempts me to despair
And tells me of the guilt within,
Upward I look and see him there
Who made an end of all my sin.
Because the sinless Saviour died
My sinful soul is counted free.
For God the just is satisfied
To look on him and pardon me.
(Charitie Lees Bancroft, 'Before the Throne of God
Above', 1863)

Day 19

Read Hebrews 10:32 – 11:40

Key verses: Hebrews 11:1–2, 6

••

¹Now faith is confidence in what we hope for and assurance about what we do not see. ²This is what the ancients were commended for . . .

⁶And without faith it is impossible to please God, because anyone who comes to him must believe that he exists and that he rewards those who earnestly seek him.

I will make you into a great nation . . . all peoples on earth will be blessed through you.
(Genesis 12:2–3)

This was God's promise to Abraham. From a human point of view it was physically impossible. Abraham was seventy-five and his wife sixty-five. She was long past childbearing age but, even if she hadn't been, the Bible tells us she was barren. Nevertheless, Abraham trusted God's promise (Hebrews 11:11; Romans 4:3).

No doubt the couple expected the promised baby to arrive in nine months, but the promise of God rang in their ears for twenty-five years before Isaac arrived. God is never in a hurry. God told Eve the seed of her womb would crush the head of the serpent. When she gave birth she said, 'I have brought forth a man', thinking that this was the promised seed to crush the head of the serpent (Genesis 4:1). They called him Cain, but he wasn't the promise at all: he became a murderer. Millennium after millennium went by before there was the cry of the baby in Bethlehem. God takes his time (see also Isaiah 5:19).

Isaac was born and grew up. No doubt Abraham anticipated he would marry at twenty, have a baby every year for the next twenty years and get this nation on the road! But he didn't marry till he was forty. Abraham had to employ a servant to find him a wife and, of all the women he could have chosen, the woman he found was barren. It was twenty years before Rebekah eventually conceived and gave birth to twins Jacob and Esau.

Abraham recognized that God often works slowly. Jesus said in John 8:56, 'Your father Abraham rejoiced at the thought of seeing my day; he saw it and was glad.' Abraham acknowledged that God's purpose and plan was something bigger than his children or grandchildren and he was to wait patiently for God to fulfil his promise.

When we walk by faith, we do not know what God is doing; we have to wait. And God takes his time. Like Abraham, we need to trust God.

Are you waiting for God to act? Waiting for him to bring your children to salvation, to vindicate you in a difficult work situation, to restore a broken relationship? Will you bring God pleasure by trusting him in these dark days (Hebrews 11:6)? Faith is being sure that God knows what he is doing. One day God's purposes will be fulfilled. The writer urges us,

> You . . . joyfully accepted [your suffering] . . . because you knew that you yourselves had better and lasting possessions. So do not throw away your confidence; it will be richly rewarded.
>
> You need to persevere so that when you have done the will of God, you will receive what he has promised. (Hebrews 10:34–36)

Day 20

Read Hebrews 10:32 – 11:40
Key verses: Hebrews 11:24–29

....

[24] By faith Moses, when he had grown up, refused to be known as the son of Pharaoh's daughter. [25] He chose to be ill-treated along with the people of God rather than to enjoy the fleeting pleasures of sin. [26] He regarded disgrace for the sake of Christ as of greater value than the treasures of Egypt, because he was looking ahead to his reward. [27] By faith he left Egypt, not fearing the king's anger; he persevered because he saw him who is invisible. [28] By faith he kept the Passover and the application of blood, so that the destroyer of the firstborn would not touch the firstborn of Israel.

[29] By faith the people passed through the Red Sea as on dry land; but when the Egyptians tried to do so, they were drowned.

At last God was going to rescue his people!

In a divine encounter at the burning bush, God told the eighty-year-old Moses that he was going to save his people (Exodus 3:7–9). The proviso was, 'I'll do it through you. You have to step out in obedience and trust me.'

So Moses did. He faced Pharaoh and eventually, after God had sent the tenth plague, the Israelites were released and Moses led them out of Egypt. When they got to the Red Sea the sea hemmed them in in front, the Egyptian army hemmed them in behind and they began to panic. They complained to Moses, who replied with the remarkable affirmation: 'Do not be afraid. Stand firm and you will see the deliverance the LORD will bring you today . . . The LORD will fight for you; you need only to be still' (Exodus 14:13–14).

This didn't mean they just stood on the banks and did nothing. God told Moses to keep the people moving and to hold out his staff over the sea all night. This must have been a strange sight, but Moses had learned that you must obey what God says and trust who God is. As God parted the waves Moses demonstrated that faith sees beyond circumstances.

You may be wondering why God has allowed a particular set of circumstances to come into your life. You want to do God's will, you are trusting his purposes, you stepped out in faith, but things have gone wrong. You are not the first to have been there. But faith sees beyond circumstances. God is going to fulfil his purpose.

Take heart from Hebrews 11. These men and women of faith did not experience one success after another. From a human perspective their lives were full of failure, conflict, difficulty and tragedy. And yet God was at work. Will you join this gallery of saints and, even when you can't see what God is doing, 'live by faith, not by sight' (2 Corinthians 5:7)? Although your circumstances may look bleak, keep on trusting who God is and obeying all that he tells you to do.

Day 21

Read Hebrews 11:1–40
Key verses: Hebrews 11:31–34

....

> [31] *By faith the prostitute Rahab, because she welcomed the spies, was not killed with those who were disobedient.*
> [32] *And what more shall I say? I do not have time to tell about Gideon, Barak, Samson and Jephthah . . .* [33] *who through faith . . . gained what was promised . . .* [34] *whose weakness was turned to strength; and who became powerful in battle and routed foreign armies.*

There are some surprising names in this Hebrews 11 list of people who lived by faith.

Rahab the prostitute is mentioned. Two spies sent to check out the land of Canaan hid in her house. She helped them escape and told them, 'I know that the LORD has given this land to you' (Joshua 2:9). She had heard about the Lord drying up the Red Sea and how the Israelites had destroyed Sihon and Og. She knew that their God was *the* God.

She spoke with certainty. She didn't know any theology. She hadn't a history of God's leading as the spies had. And yet this prostitute took God at his word.

Samson too had messed up his life. He was one of the judges. He was born to be a Nazirite, which meant he was not supposed to drink wine, go near a dead body or cut his hair. But he broke all those vows. His big problem was his promiscuity; he fell easily in and out of love. He fell in love with Delilah and foolishly told her the secret of his strength. Eventually the Philistines captured him, gouged out his eyes and locked him up. In his cell his hair, which had been cut off, grew again and God restored his strength. When he was brought into the temple he prayed, 'God, just one more time, give me strength.' He pushed against the pillars and brought the building down, killing himself and the others inside (Judges 16). The whole story of Samson is tragic, but despite his weakness and his failings he trusted God and is listed in this catalogue of those who lived by faith.

In 2 Chronicles 16:9 it says, 'The eyes of the LORD run to and fro throughout the whole earth, to show Himself strong on behalf of those whose heart is loyal to Him' (NKJV). God is looking for those who will let him show himself strong on their behalf.

That's why Rahab and Samson make the list.

Your life may have fallen apart for all kinds of reasons. Your failings and flaws may be obvious for all to see. God is not looking for you to be the finished article. The Holy Spirit will work at producing fruit in you and making you more like Christ. But, in the meantime, you can trust God. Ask God to demonstrate *his* strength in and through your life. Today, pray, 'God, I take you at your word. I trust in you.'

Day 22

Read Hebrews 11:1–40
Key verses: Hebrews 11:35–40

....

[35] Women received back their dead, raised to life again. There were others who were tortured, refusing to be released so that they might gain an even better resurrection. [36] Some faced jeers and flogging, and even chains and imprisonment. [37] They were put to death by stoning; they were sawn in two; they were killed by the sword. They went about in sheepskins and goatskins, destitute, persecuted and ill-treated – [38] the world was not worthy of them. They wandered in deserts and mountains, living in caves and in holes in the ground.

[39] These were all commended for their faith, yet none of them received what had been promised, [40] since God had planned something better for us so that only together with us would they be made perfect.

Don't get the idea that if you have faith in God you'll avoid all hardships in life; that you'll never get sick, never get down, never be depressed and never be hurt.

We might be forgiven for assuming from the earlier verses that faith in God means, ultimately, we're never beaten, we're not overcome and we don't really get hurt – but that's not true. The writer to the Hebrews gives examples of people commended for their faith who died, were persecuted and suffered.

Stephen is the first martyr recorded in the book of Acts. As he was being stoned to death, he looked up and saw Jesus, standing at the right hand of the Father. Normally Jesus is portrayed as sitting at the Father's right hand. Some have said he was standing to welcome the martyr home. Maybe. But although Stephen saw Jesus standing at the right hand of the Father, Jesus didn't intervene. He saw Stephen's blood-soaked face and he didn't rescue him. God allowed the death of Stephen. Among other things he was sowing seeds in Saul of Tarsus that day. That arch-enemy of the church would later become a Christian and a great champion of the gospel.

Like Stephen in the New Testament, these characters from the Old Testament in Hebrews 11 didn't escape conflict and tragedies, but they persevered through them by faith, trusting that God had a plan.

We too need to trust that there is a bigger picture than the limited aspects we can see.

Remember, if without faith it is impossible to please God, then the reverse is also true – with faith it is impossible *not* to please God. You can go to bed tonight and say, 'I may have had a rough day, a day I would not like to live through again, but I know I've lived today in dependence on him, trusting him to work out his purpose. Faith is being sure of what we hope for. It may not be in my hand now, but I know that God is going to bring about his work; he's going to accomplish his purpose.'

Will you trust God like this and join the list of those commended for their faith?

Day 23

Read Hebrews 11:32 – 12:1
Key verse: Hebrews 12:1

....

¹Therefore, since we are surrounded by such a great cloud of witnesses, let us throw off everything that hinders and the sin that so easily entangles. And let us run with perseverance the race marked out for us.

There are only two options in the Christian life: you either press on to maturity or you subject the Son of God to public disgrace (Hebrews 6:1–6).

Pressing on to maturity is the appeal not only in chapter 6 but throughout the book, and it is here again in chapter 12.

How are we to mature? The writer tells us to look around at the cloud of witnesses he has described in chapter 11. These individuals experienced God and they are witnesses to us of God's sufficiency in times of need. If you are facing a big problem, go back to Abraham and ask: how did he trust God? How did Moses trust God? How did these men and women of Hebrews 11 trust God? Then you can ask the question: how am I to trust God in the light of their example?

The writer is saying, 'You are not the first one on this journey. You are not the first one to face troubles and temptations. I've given you a catalogue of just some of the people from the past who knew God. They are witnesses to us that he is the same yesterday, today and for ever' (see Hebrews 13:8).'

Don't look at the past with rose-tinted glasses. These characters from the chapter of faith experienced obstacles, temptations, frustrations and almost constant battle. They are reminders to us that God does his best work in tough situations. Again and again he proves his sufficiency to us when we are at the end of our own resources.

Their God is our God.

Think about the Bible heroes who have inspired you and also the individuals who have been influential in your own spiritual journey. What have you learned about being faithful to God and about God's sufficiency from watching their lives? Thank God for these men and women, and realize that, like you, they have faced troubles and temptations. Reflect on how they dealt with these crises. How can you depend on the resources they relied upon?

Remember, their God is your God. So trust God's unchangeable character and his bountiful sufficiency. 'Anything God has ever done, He can do now. Anything God has ever done anywhere, He can do here. Anything God has ever done for anyone, He can do for you' (A. W. Tozer, quoted in *Leadership Weekly*, 9 October 2002). Just think: even today your life could be a witness testimony to God's sufficiency, spurring someone else on in the faith.

Day 24

Read Hebrews 11:23–28; 12:1
Key verse: Hebrews 12:1

••

[1] Therefore, since we are surrounded by such a great cloud of witnesses, let us throw off everything that hinders and the sin that so easily entangles. And let us run with perseverance the race marked out for us.

Have you heard any sermons about 'throwing off' recently?

'Throwing off' the things that entangle us is not something we hear a lot about these days. We want to be positive and affirm the good without exposing the bad. Yes, the gospel is positive, but self-denial is every bit as much a part of Christian experience as living in the fullness of God. Taking up the cross is as much a part of the Christian life as enjoying his resurrection life. Brokenness is God's agenda for us as a prelude to wholeness. Dying with Christ is necessary that we might live with him. Too often we want the benefits without the obligations.

Hebrews 12 talks about the things we need to throw off. Look at just one example from the life of Moses. He refused to be known as the son of Pharaoh's daughter (Hebrews 11:24–25). Having been adopted into the royal family of one of the greatest nations on earth, he had all the privileges of such a position laid at his feet, but he denied himself those privileges – not because they were in themselves wrong, but because they would interfere with God's purpose for him. That's why Hebrews makes this analogy of running the race. There is nothing wrong with big boots, but you don't wear them when you are running a race. There is nothing wrong with a heavy coat, but don't wear it if you want to reach the finish line. And there are things in life which are not intrinsically wrong, but aren't good when measured against bigger criteria: 'What enables me to further God's interest, God's purpose, God's agenda in my life?' Because what hinders his purpose and agenda, what impedes my growth in holiness, may not be wrong for somebody else, but it needs to come out of my life.

We tend to rate our spiritual life according to what we see in the people around us. We use the lives of our friends to gauge how well we are doing spiritually. If we're going to the same number of services, have the same standard of living, use the same language, then we must be doing all right. But Hebrews says you are to run the race God marked out for *you* – not for someone else. Is there something morally neutral, or even good, which is hindering God's purpose or agenda for your life? An attachment to family ties when God is asking you to serve him overseas? A desire to be comfortable instead of giving sacrificially? It might be a small thing: God nudging you to do a Bible study when you meet with your friend, instead of just having a coffee and a chat. What is impeding your holiness?

Day 25

Read Hebrews 11:24–25; 12:14–17

Key verse: Hebrews 12:16

••

¹⁶See that no one is sexually immoral, or is godless like Esau, who for a single meal sold his inheritance rights as the oldest son.

Sin is pleasurable.

That's why we have a problem with it. If sin wasn't enjoyable and attractive we wouldn't be tempted by it. We face a continual struggle to live beyond satisfying our senses and succumbing to the popular motto 'If it feels good, do it'.

You can imagine the pleasures of sin Moses could have enjoyed growing up in the royal palace. No doubt he could have clicked his fingers and got any girl or anything else he wanted. But he recognized that pleasure was fleeting, lasting only a season, and he was committed to serving God for life. So he denied himself the pleasures of sin, choosing instead to be ill-treated by the Egyptians alongside the Israelites.

We think of sex as the big 'lust of the flesh' to avoid, but, if you look carefully in the Bible, you may discover that food is. In the Garden of Eden Eve ate the forbidden fruit. Esau, for a plate of food, lost his birthright. The Israelites wanted to return to captivity in Egypt because they missed the food! 'If only we had meat to eat! We remember the fish we ate in Egypt at no cost – also the cucumbers, melons, leeks, onions and garlic' (Numbers 11:4–5). The first temptation Satan gave Jesus was, 'If you are the Son of God, tell these stones to become bread' (Matthew 4:3).

Food and sex have many similarities. Both relate to physical appetites which, if not kept under control, can lead us into sin. Here the writer associates Esau's loss of his birthright for a plate of food with sexual immorality. Both are legitimate appetites we are tempted to fulfil illegitimately.

In our day, the anonymity, accessibility and affordability of Internet pornography make it highly addictive. This sin is rampant among Christians as well as non-Christians. Again, it is appealing illegitimately to a legitimate sexual appetite. But it will entangle and destroy you. (For further information and help, see *The Porn Problem* by Vaughan Roberts, The Good Book Company, forthcoming, 2018.)

Whatever your particular sin, whatever vulnerability you face, look back to the great cloud of witnesses. Their God is your God. He was sufficient for them, and he will be sufficient for you.

> The great enemy of the gospel puts the question to us every day, 'Shall we continue to sin?' You and I need to be talking to ourselves, and saying, 'But don't you know that you are one with Christ; that you have died to sin, and risen to God? Don't you know that you are a slave to God, and committed therefore to obedience? Don't you know these things?' And go on asking yourself that question until you reply to yourself, 'Yes I do know. And by the grace of God I shall live accordingly.'
> (John Stott, *The Keswick Week 1965*, Marshall, Morgan & Scott, 1965, pp. 65–66)

Day 26

Read Hebrews 12:1–29
Key verses: Hebrews 12:1–2

. . . .

¹Let us run with perseverance the race marked out for us, ²fixing our eyes on Jesus, the pioneer and perfecter of faith. For the joy that was set before him he endured the cross, scorning its shame, and sat down at the right hand of the throne of God.

What do you focus your attention and energies on?

In Hebrews 3:1 the writer urges us, 'Fix your thoughts on Jesus.' Here in 12:2 the charge is, 'Fix your eyes on Jesus.' The context is the catalogue in chapter 11 of people who lived by faith. Then the writer says that Jesus is the 'pioneer and perfecter of faith' – or, as the New King James Version puts it, 'the author and finisher of our faith'. The object in whom we place our faith is Christ. He is therefore both the beginner of our faith and, as he goes on being the object in whom we place our trust, the finisher of our faith.

If we are going to grow and mature in the Christian life we don't move beyond Christ to something more! Every day we live in fresh dependence on him. It follows, therefore, that the more you fix your attention on him, the more you get to know him and the more you're going to trust him. The reason why we don't trust God is, very simply, because we don't know him well enough. The more we get to know him, the easier it becomes to trust him.

One of the most important things in the Christian life is getting to know God better, supremely by getting to know Christ. That's why we read the Bible: not to get to know the Bible, but to get to know Christ. The more confident we are of the object of our faith, the less conscious we are of the faith itself. If you had the option of making a long journey in either a brand-new BMW or a forty-year-old VW Beetle and you chose the Beetle, someone might commend you for having a lot of faith! If you chose the BMW no-one would mention your faith – because the more confident we are in the object of our faith, the less conscious we are of the faith itself. The more we know God, the less conscious we are of any risk element and the fact that we live by faith.

Alec Motyer said of Epaphroditus, the gospel worker who delivered Paul's letter to the Philippians: 'He took a calculated risk, involving the expenditure of all he had, relying only on the trustworthiness of Jesus Christ. He staked all on Jesus, knowing that he could not fail' (*The Richness of Christ*, IVP, 1966). What is stopping you expending all that you have for Christ? Do you need to get to know him better? Do you need to get rid of distractions and fix your eyes on him more intently? Ask the Holy Spirit to help you be obedient to God and 'do whatever he tells you' (John 2:5).

Day 27

Read Hebrews 12:1–29
Key verses: Hebrews 12:1–3

••

> ¹*Let us run with perseverance the race marked out for us,* ²*fixing our eyes on Jesus, the pioneer and perfecter of faith. For the joy that was set before him he endured the cross, scorning its shame, and sat down at the right hand of the throne of God.* ³*Consider him who endured such opposition from sinners, so that you will not grow weary and lose heart.*

The Christian Gospel is that I am so flawed that Jesus had to die for me, yet I am so loved and valued that Jesus was glad to die for me.
(Tim Keller, *The Reason for God: Belief in an Age of Scepticism*, Hodder and Stoughton, 2009 p. 179)

Christ went gladly and willingly to the cross for you. But don't ever get the idea he went waltzing to the cross saying, 'Oh well, this is all par for the course.' In the Garden of Gethsemane he said, 'Father, if it is possible for this cup to be taken from me, if there's any other way that a man or woman, a boy or girl can be reconciled to a holy God; if there's any other way, please let that be the way; but if there is no other way, your will be done.' In such a spirit he went to the cross and endured the agony.

We might speculate about the physical agony, but we can't even begin to understand the spiritual agony Jesus suffered. He cried out in anguish, 'My God, my God, why have you forsaken me?' (Matthew 27:46). The very atmosphere of hell descended on him in those hours of darkness. Why did he do it? The writer to the Hebrews says it was 'for the joy that was set before him'.

What was the joy set before him? The prophetic statement about the cross in Isaiah 53 helps us to understand. Verse 11 says, 'He shall see of the travail of his soul, and shall be satisfied' (KJV). You and I were the joy set before him. Jesus endured the cross for the joy of knowing that human beings might be redeemed and reconciled to God.

The cross demonstrates just how much Christ loves you.

Difficult circumstances often leave us questioning God's love. We say to ourselves, 'If God really loved me, surely he would take this cup of suffering away from me?' Hebrews 12:2 confronts us with the startling truth: God loves you with an unfailing, everlasting, Calvary love. Before you were even born, Jesus knew you. He endured the agony of the cross because his mind was fixed on you and on how you could be reconciled to God. Today you may endure suffering, but trust him in dark days, knowing you are known, loved and cared for. This truth can thrill your heart and spur you on to greater devotion.

I have loved you with an everlasting love;
I have drawn you with unfailing kindness.
(Jeremiah 31:3)

Day 28

Read Hebrews 12:4–29
Key verses: Hebrews 12:5–7

....

> [5]*And have you completely forgotten this word of encouragement that addresses you as a father addresses his son? It says,*
>> *'My son, do not make light of the Lord's discipline,*
>> *and do not lose heart when he rebukes you,*
>> [6]*because the Lord disciplines the one he loves,*
>> *and he chastens everyone he accepts as his son.'*
> [7]*Endure hardship as discipline; God is treating you as his children. For what children are not disciplined by their father?*

When life is tough we are tempted to assume something is wrong with us. We may be embarrassed about our financial struggles, job uncertainty, physical suffering or strained relationships. We worry that our troubles might be a sign of our own failure, lack of faith or disobedience.

But hardship is not something to be embarrassed about. Suffering is a fact of life and one of the ways God teaches and moulds us. Like a loving parent God disciplines us for good (verse 7). We don't look for suffering, but again and again it is God's agent for good in our lives. Through it we discover what real values are, and through it God may conform us to the image of Jesus. 'It is good for a man to bear the yoke while he is young' (Lamentations 3:27). Suffering is productive; it produces 'perseverance; perseverance, character; and character, hope' (Romans 5:3–4).

Philippians 1:29 reminds us that suffering for Christ is part of the package of Christianity: 'For it has been granted to you on behalf of Christ not only to believe in him, but also to suffer for him.' We don't suffer in spite of God's will because we live in a fallen environment; we suffer according to God's will: 'So then, those who suffer according to God's will should commit themselves to their faithful Creator and continue to do good' (1 Peter 4:19). In a mysterious way suffering can be a prelude to glory, the foretaste of great blessing to come (Romans 8:17–18).

As we mature in Christ we look at the situations and hardships of life that we come up against and allow them to be God's tool moulding us into richer, deeper people, as he intends.

Don't despise your suffering. Instead, pray that God would help you see your circumstances as he does.

No wound? No scar?
Yet, as the Master shall the servant be,
And pierced are the feet that follow Me;
But thine are whole: can he have followed far
Who has nor wound nor scar?
(Amy Carmichael, *Toward Jerusalem: Poems of Faith*, SPCK, 1936)

Friends, when life gets really difficult, don't jump to the conclusion that God isn't on the job. Instead, be glad that you are in the very thick of what Christ experienced. This is a spiritual refining process, with glory just around the corner.
(1 Peter 4:12–13, MSG)

Day 29

Read Hebrews 12:4–29
Key verses: Hebrews 12:10–11

....

> ¹⁰ *They [human fathers] disciplined us for a little while as they thought best; but God disciplines us for our good, in order that we may share in his holiness.* ¹¹ *No discipline seems pleasant at the time, but painful. Later on, however, it produces a harvest of righteousness and peace for those who have been trained by it.*

Hope is essential to life.

We orientate our life around a future hope, a high expectation or a longing. It may be something as trivial as a holiday, or it may be watching our children and perhaps grandchildren grow up. Looking forward in hope is one of the ingredients of a healthy life, materially and spiritually. It alters how we feel about the present.

This theme of looking forward runs throughout this whole letter. Go back to Hebrews 11:10 and Abraham is 'looking forward to the city with foundations, whose architect and builder is God'. Hebrews 11:16 says that the men and women were listed here 'longing for a better country'. Moses, too, was looking ahead to his reward; that's why he chose the disgrace of the people of God. The goal that kept them looking forward and pressing on is explained in Hebrews 12:10: 'God disciplines us for our good, in order that we may share in his holiness.' Sharing the holiness of God is our ultimate hope, for it alone brings deep satisfaction to our souls.

Hope in the Bible is a confident expectation based not on wishful thinking, but on the revelation God has given us in his Word.

No matter what situation we are in, through faith we can look beyond our circumstances and say, 'There is a city, whose foundation and builder is God. There is a future for which I am being prepared. It is a journey it is impossible to fall away from, for we have been eternally sealed in that journey by the Holy Spirit.'

The writer to the Hebrews describes our hope in Christ as 'an anchor for the soul, firm and secure' (Hebrews 6:19). Whatever troubles are swirling around you right now, let your hope in Christ and all that God has planned for you hold you fast. Draw peace and strength from knowing that your future is secure. God's glorious plan and purpose for you will be fulfilled.

> Therefore we do not lose heart. Though outwardly we are wasting away, yet inwardly we are being renewed day by day. For our light and momentary troubles are achieving for us an eternal glory that far outweighs them all. So we fix our eyes not on what is seen, but on what is unseen, since what is seen is temporary, but what is unseen is eternal.
> (2 Corinthians 4:16–18)

> May the God of hope fill you with all joy and peace as you trust in him, so that you may overflow with hope by the power of the Holy Spirit.
> (Romans 15:13)

Day 30

Read Hebrews 13:1–25
Key verses: Hebrews 13:20–21

. . . .

[20] Now may the God of peace, who through the blood of the eternal covenant brought back from the dead our Lord Jesus, that great Shepherd of the sheep, [21] equip you with everything good for doing his will, and may he work in us what is pleasing to him, through Jesus Christ, to whom be glory for ever and ever. Amen.

Perhaps more than ever before people are watching to see whether our lives express our beliefs. Many are sick of outward pretence and genuinely hunger for authenticity and integrity.

The author of Hebrews knew the value of practical Christian living and describes what spiritual maturity looks like. After all the teaching and warnings, the letter concludes with loving application. The issues that were prevalent in the church then – sex, money, power, suffering and worship –

are still hot topics today. Yet, despite the cultural norms and pressure to conform in our own particular society, the writer urges us to live distinctive lives explicable only by the work and presence of God within us.

Whether talking about being content and not loving money (verse 5) or about obeying our leaders (verse 7), he explains that the motivation for our behaviour is God living within us. Throughout the chapter Jesus' supremacy – and his role as mediator of the new covenant and pioneer of faith who is always available to his people – is the focus.

The great promise is that the God who guided the Israelites in the days of the old covenant, who intercedes for us today and who will take us to 'the city that is to come', is unchanged and unchangeable. 'Jesus Christ is the same yesterday and today and for ever' (verse 8). He is completely trustworthy, and if our faith is firmly rooted in him we can be sustained and guided through difficult times (verses 5–6).

Yes, we have to be diligent and persevere, but even as we do so God is at work in us and through us. As this prayer of blessing in verses 20–21 highlights, spiritual growth is possible. We have the God who planned and brought about our salvation and who raised Jesus from the dead, and the living Lord Jesus who guides and keeps us, and who gave us the Holy Spirit, to equip us and enable all that God has called us to be and to do.

What grace!

Perhaps God is asking you to step out into a whole new area of service. Perhaps he is challenging you about your spiritual growth. Whatever he is calling you to be or to do, press on with confidence. Obey wholeheartedly, knowing that God will keep his promise to equip and enable you.

> May God, who puts all things together,
>   makes all things whole,
> Who made a lasting mark through the sacrifice of
>   Jesus,
>   the sacrifice of blood that sealed the eternal
>   covenant,
> Who led Jesus, our Great Shepherd,
>   up and alive from the dead,
> Now put you together, provide you
>   with everything you need to please him,
> Make us into what gives him most pleasure,
>   by means of the sacrifice of Jesus, the Messiah.
> All glory to Jesus forever and always!
>   Oh, yes, yes, yes.
> (Hebrews 13:20–21, MSG)

For further study

If you would like to do further study on Hebrews, the following commentaries may be useful:

- Raymond Brown, *The Message of Hebrews*, The Bible Speaks Today (IVP, 2000).

- F. F. Bruce, *The Epistle to the Hebrews*, New International Commentary on the New Testament (Eerdmans, Revised edition, 2011).

- George H. Guthrie, *Hebrews*, NIV Application Commentary (Zondervan, 1998).

- Tom Wright, *Hebrews for Everyone* (SPCK, 2003).

KESWICK MINISTRIES

Our purpose

Keswick Ministries is committed to the spiritual renewal of God's people for his mission in the world.

God's purpose is to bring his blessing to all the nations of the world. That promise of blessing, which touches every aspect of human life, is ultimately fulfilled through the life, death, resurrection, ascension and future return of Christ. All of the people of God are called to participate in his missionary purposes, wherever he may place them. The central vision of Keswick Ministries is to see the people of God equipped, encouraged and refreshed to fulfil that calling, directed and guided by God's Word in the power of his Spirit, for the glory of his Son.

Our priorities

Keswick Ministries seeks to serve the local church through:

- *Hearing God's Word*: the Scriptures are the foundation for the church's life, growth and mission, and Keswick Ministries is committed to preaching and teaching God's Word in a way that is faithful to Scripture and relevant to Christians of all ages and backgrounds.

- *Becoming like God's Son*: from its earliest days the Keswick movement has encouraged Christians to live godly lives in the power of the Spirit, to grow in Christ-likeness and to live under his lordship in every area of life. This is God's will for his people in every culture and generation.

- *Serving God's mission*: the authentic response to God's Word is obedience to his mission, and the inevitable result of Christlikeness is sacrificial service. Keswick Ministries seeks to encourage committed discipleship in family life, work and society, and energetic engagement in the cause of world mission.

Our ministry

- *Keswick: the event.* Every summer the town of Keswick hosts a three-week convention, which attracts some 15,000 Christians from the UK and around the world. The event provides Bible teaching for all ages, vibrant worship, a sense of unity across generations and denominations, and an inspirational call to serve Christ in the world. It caters for children of all ages and has a strong youth and young adult programme. And it all takes place in the beautiful Lake District – a perfect setting for rest, recreation and refreshment.

- *Keswick: the movement.* For 140 years the work of Keswick has had an impact on churches worldwide, and today the movement is underway throughout the UK, as well as in many parts of Europe, Asia, North America, Australia, Africa and the Caribbean. Keswick Ministries is committed to strengthening the network in the UK and beyond, through prayer, news, pioneering and cooperative activity.

- *Keswick resources.* Keswick Ministries produces a range of books and booklets based on the core foundations of Christian life and mission. It makes Bible teaching available through free access to mp3 downloads, and the sale of DVDs and CDs. It broadcasts online through Clayton TV and annual BBC Radio 4 services.

- *Keswick teaching and training.* In addition to the summer convention, Keswick Ministries is developing teaching and training events that will happen at other times of the year and in other places.

Our unity

The Keswick movement worldwide has adopted a key Pauline statement to describe its gospel inclusivity: 'for you are all one in Christ Jesus' (Galatians 3:28). Keswick Ministries works with evangelicals from a wide variety of church backgrounds, on the understanding that they share a commitment to the essential truths of the Christian faith as set out in its statement of belief.

Our contact details
T: 01768 780075
E: info@keswickministries.org
W: www.keswickministries.org
Mail: Keswick Ministries, Convention Centre, Skiddaw Street, Keswick CA12 4BY, England

Related titles from IVP

Related teaching CD packs

Ezekiel
Liam Goligher
SWP2263D (5-CD pack)
SWP2263A (5-DVD pack)

Hebrews
Charles Price
SWP2281D (5-CD pack)

ALSO AVAILABLE

SWP2203D
(5-CD pack)

SWP2202D
(4-CD pack)

SWP2239D
(4-CD pack)

SWP2238D
(5-CD pack)

SWP2238A
(5-DVD pack)

SWP2280
(5-CD pac

SWP2280
(5-DVD pa

Available from www.essentialchristian.com